GET RICH QUICK

HOW TO MAKE MONEY ONLINE

TIMOTHY WELLS

CONTENTS

INTRODUCTION

Welcome to the information age. In a world where information can freely travel from across the globe, anyone with internet access can be updated with what the latest information can offer.

The world's economy is becoming more unstable, the population blooms, and job security is close to non-existent. While the majority of the planet still firmly believes in working for money, some actually take advantage of doing the opposite; letting money work for them. This is why a number of business-minded individuals become interested in growing their own businesses.

The internet offers a lot of opportunities for people, just like you, to earn income and grow a business. However, making money online is not easy, but I hope that you are able to use this as a guide to spark a ton of new ideas for you to make a living online. It may take a year or more to establish a working, online business model. But once you find the business model that works for you, it can be a very rewarding experience.

The basic idea of any form of business is to work

extremely hard now, and continually reap the benefits later. And yes, this can be accomplished.

This book covers a variety of different things from ideas and websites, to spending smart, as well as the strategies people use to get rich.

Let's begin!

1

THE MINDSET YOU NEED TO HAVE TO MAKE A LIVING ONLINE

There are endless opportunities when it comes to making money online. One of the biggest advantages of online businesses is that you have the opportunity to work at home. They can save on transportation costs and most importantly, they allow you to spend more time with your families, earn a passive income, and travel the world.

To be a successful entrepreneur you must and have the courage to innovate and try something new. One must conduct extensive research about how they're going to start. Making money online can be very rewarding in itself and challenging at the same time because like any entrepreneur you will need to "find the right shoe that fits" and therefore go through some trial and error. Throughout this book you will be provided with shortcuts to make this process much easier, saving you tons of time.

A book that many people have found useful is Michael Greene's Bestseller, *How To Make Money Without Having A Job*, where he includes over 50 of the best websites to begin making money from home.

If you want o know more about how to have a "Think Rich" Mindset, I recommend Michael Edwards' book, Think Rich. It gives strategies for using the Law of Attraction to your advantage because the biggest part of the money making game is the mind.

INCOME FROM THE INTERNET

In the business world, there are three identified types of income; active or earned income, portfolio income, and passive income.

Active or earned income is the money you earn from hours of work. Income that you receive that is directly dependent on the work hours you've done is called active income.

Passive income is characterized by the ability to generate wealth without your constant attention. It continues to generate wealth for you while you sleep, eat, watch movies, and go on holidays. Of course, you'll need to put extra hard work when setting up your business assets and occasionally check or review your assets.

On the internet, the number one source of passive income is through advertisements. You won't have to worry about the advertisements firsthand. Advertisements will be provided by affiliate/partnership programs such as Google Adsense, and Amazon Associates. Your job will be to construct the page where the ads will be visible. It could be a blog, a video upload, an online article, or an entire website. It is also your job to increase the visitors to your page.

Through advertisements, your earnings can be determined based on how many people clicked on your site's ads. So to put it simply, the only way to generate more profits through ads is to increase the amount of traffic that your page receives.

Amazon Affiliate Marketing by Michael Greene which goes into detail about how to get started making by promoting amazon products on a website or blog you create.

Portfolio income is the profit you receive from investments, dividends, interest, royalties and capital gains. However, investments made to businesses do not yield portfolio income; instead, they are considered as passive income. The investments that give you portfolio income are investments in stocks, bonds, currencies, futures, mutual funds, and more. In Todd Williams book, *The Secret Guide To Making Money With Investments*, he talks about how to outperform most professional investors, how to double your money, as well as the advantages/disadvantages of different types of investments to help you decide what to invest in.

In making money online, you'll be focusing on generating passive and portfolio income, depending on the online strategy you're going to use. Passive and portfolio income is the kind of income you need in order to gain wealth.

*Or if you want to get the whole shebang, I highly recommend Michael Greene's Bestseller, Make Money Online: Start A Business, which covers all the topics of making money online and online marketing too.

A SMART DOMAIN NAME

Domain names are considered the real estate of the internet. A domain name is a string of characters followed by top-level domains (TLD) like .com, .org, .net, etc. A domain name is used only to identify a location on the internet, which means that a domain name can exist without a website. This concept is called 'domain parking'. Visiting an empty domain name usually displays an 'incomplete' website that usually contains advertising listings or links.

The owner of the domain name usually gets paid for each links clicked by visitors. This commissions system is called 'pay-per-click'. The links and listings displayed on the site are generated based on the predicted topic or interest that the visitors click on. A parked domain's value can be determined by the amount of visitors it gets. Most of the time, this amount is recorded in a monthly basis. Therefore, domain names can be your virtual assets for your online business.

Domain names can be monetized through links. Domain names can also be bought or sold, depending on the demand for the domain. The process of trading domain names is facilitated in 'Domain name auctions'. Websites such as www.auctions.godaddy.com and www.sedo.com are examples of domain auction websites.

In order to participate in the domain name marketplace, one must know how to own domain names first. Domain names must be registered at domain registrars. Here is a list of the most used domain name registrars on the internet:

1. **iPage** – www.ipage.com
2. **justhost.com** – www.justhost.com
3. **web.com** – www.web.com
4. **Network Solutions** – www.networksolutions.com
5. **Bluehost** – www.bluehost.com
6. **Host Gator** – www.hostgator.com
7. **FatCow** – www.fatcow.com
8. **1 & 1** – www.1and1.com
9. **Hub** – www.webhostinghub.com
10. **GoDaddy** – www.godaddy.com

*TIPS IN CREATING **domain names***

1. Only opt for the '.com' Top Level Domain
2. - The potential traffic of the domain name you're planning should be your top priority. The TLD '.com' is what the majority of the internet use. You can even say that some people think that all web addresses end with a '.com'.
3. Look out for copyrights

4. - Be sure that you're not violating anyone's copyright when naming your domain. A copyright infringement, especially with bigger companies, usually ends up with a lawsuit. And it will cost you money. So before choosing your domain name, double check for possible copyrights you could be violating.

5. Make it short

6. - Create short domain names that are easy to remember. Whether you're running a fully-operational website or just hosting a parked domain, it lives and dies by the visitors. Shorter names can also be easily typed, so there's a bigger chance for new visitors to come to your domain.

7. Choose your keywords

8. - Make sure that your domain name is directly related to the content or the niche you're after. For example; if you want to create a cooking related domain, write down 'fry, sauté, kitchen, chef, knife, chop, etc'. Then you can mix and match these words to come up with a short, but catchy domain name. Keywords play a crucial role when it comes to search engine optimization (SEO). They help improve your domain name's ranking on search engines.

9. Use simpler words

10. - The domain name marketplace isn't a spelling contest. Go with simple and easy to type words. If you want to have more visitors, make sure that it is convenient to type in your web address. There's nothing wrong with being a little creative or clever, but play it safe and don't overdress your domain name.

11. Creating a 'for sale' banner
12. - If your domain name is for sale, then it is a good
    idea to display a 'for sale' banner on your site's
    home page. Potential buyers sometimes type-in
    the domain names they want. If your domain
    name comes up, the next thing they want to
    know is if the domain name is for sale. Thanks to
    the conveniently placed 'for sale' banner, you've
    made the transaction easier.

A WELL-CHOSEN domain name is a big factor when it comes
to traffic generation. It might as well be the single deciding
factor whether you're going to succeed in domain trading or
not. D particularly helpful is having a domain name
EXACTLY like the search term you'd use in Google, such as
HowToBecomeWealthy.com the opportunities for making
money with domain names are not limited to just creating
them. Millions of domain names are available for sale on
sites like www.sedo.com. And just like real estate, domain
name trading can also yield big returns. The most successful
domain name sales are worth millions, the highest being
www.vacationrentals.com, selling for a whopping $35
million.

The next most important part about domain name
selling is pricing. You don't want to scare away potential
buyers by overpricing, or lose money by under-pricing.
There are some things you can do if you have no clue about
how much you should sell your domain name for. The first
step you should take is the free approach. You can post at
forums such as www.namepros.com and www.dnforum.com

and get some of the people's opinion whether your domain name is worthless or is the next million dollar deal.

If you want an even more in depth evaluation of your domain name, then you can try 'domain appraisal'. Some domain name sites offer domain appraisal services. This, however, is not free. The advantage of using domain appraisal services is that they can directly provide you with a calculated estimate of your domain name's price. Also, some domain appraisals provide a complete analysis of your domain value, a list of recent comparable sales, and even marketing strategy. This is optional but it can be an excellent tool when you're trying to succeed in domain name trading.

Still, it's not risk free and selling domains may take a very long time for you to get results. Learning the ways of domain name trading maybe hard but it can be very rewarding. Just be careful not to get ahead of yourself. Domain registrars charge a hosting fee for your domains. Other domain sites also have features like the 'featured domain listing', where you can get more exposure for your domain names, for a price. It may be necessary to spend an indefinite amount of money in order to get results, so tread carefully.

HOW TO GENERATE A PASSIVE INCOME ONLINE

Generating passive income from online media is one of the things that you need to do if you want to achieve financial freedom. Imagine a life where you can do all the things you want, like skiing, hiking, camping, partying, or absolutely anything you want while your online assets continue to make money for you. This is not fantasy; it is indeed possible on the internet. But the reality is, it very difficult to achieve. You'll need tremendous amounts of research, planning, and luck. There's no such thing as earning thousands of dollars overnight, but there are ways to make you rich faster. All websites claiming that they can make you rich within a week or even a day are nothing but hoaxes. Nothing comes without a price. To achieve financial success on the internet, you'll need to invest time, hard work, knowledge, and a little money.

ONLINE ADVERTISEMENTS

Virtual assets such as parked domain names, YouTube videos, and online articles can be monetized and generate passive income. The main or perhaps the only source of passive income on the internet is revenue from online advertisements. Advertisements can be promoted in your content or website by your affiliates. Your revenue can be determined on how many visitors click on an ad, or how many visitors from your website purchase the affiliated product or service. This depends on the policy of the affiliate program you choose. This is called affiliate marketing – which Patrick Kennedy goes into much more detail in his book *Make A Ton of Money With Affiliate Marketing.*

There are a lot of different affiliate marketing sites available on the internet. To name a few, we have Commission Junction (www.cj.com), Click2Sell (www.click2sell.eu), and Clickbank (www.clickbank.com). To learn more about the Clickbank, the worlds largest online marketplace where you can become an affiliate and make money selling other people's product's online, check out Michael Greene's *Make Money With Clickbank.*

The first thing you'll need to do is to choose your market niche. This is important so you can pinpoint your targeted traffic. A market niche could be about gaming, entertainment, technology, political, art, cooking, fitness, or just about anything. It is important to choose a niche you are familiar with, for the quality of the content you will be making depends on it. A specified market niche is also crucial for your success with keywords. And in turn, keywords are crucial for your success with generating traffic. However, a market can be too saturated for you to be able to get substantial results. This means that most of the good ideas are already taken, competition is tough, and market shares are limited. So sometimes, you should be more flexible and be able to explore different niches.

Once you've chosen a market niche, the next step would be to research more about niche. This is important for the quality of content you will be providing. Be sure that you're updated with the most recent information regarding your selected market niche. Always choose to get information from the most reliable sources. Your job is to be able to provide accurate, non-bogus information for your targeted traffic. Once you've set your market niche and gathered solid knowledge about it, it's time to create your content.

WRITING KINDLE BOOKS, ARTICLES, BLOGS

Writing articles and blogs online has been one of the most popular ways to generate passive income on the internet. There's a lot of different websites where you can write articles and blogs for free. These websites automatically presents ads that may be directly related to the content of your article or blog. The writer of the content can earn commission from the revenue generated through the ads, but sometimes websites offer a unique compensation system. Here is a list of reliable websites that offer compensation for their writers:

1. Bukisa.com
2. - Articles posted here must first be reviewed and approved by the Bukisa team. Once approved, you get paid via their revenue sharing system.
3. eHow.com
4. - One of the popular places to go to when someone wants to know how to do something. This is great for people who are good at creating

instructional materials such as how to cook, repair something, etc.

5. Hubpages.com
6. - Hubpages allows writers to create their content by using the online editor. Authors can associate their content with Google Adsense and Amazon. If you'd like more information on Amazon Associates and to be taken step-by-step to making money with Amazon Marketing, this book is great to get started: Amazon Affiliate Marketing
7. Squidoo.com
8. - Squidoo is an easy to use platform that is widely used by many people for promoting their products, interests, and websites. It lets you create mini-sites of your own. They call these 'lenses'. It also offers a lot of earning programs for authors who are interested on monetizing their content.
9. Ezinearticles.com
10. - Ezine articles also known as electronic magazine, is one of the most popular article websites today and ranked in the top 5 for its generated traffic daily. Articles submitted are reviewed twice. Authors with remarkable content are rewarded a platinum membership that allows them to submit unlimited articles and top priority when it comes to their submissions.

WRITING articles online and monetizing its content is one of the cheapest ways on making money online. These websites offer aspiring authors the ability to post their works for free and offer a variety of earning programs such as the pay-per-click, and banner advertising for other website owners. Article websites tend to have a higher page rank than blogs, which means it has a higher probability of being shown on the first or second page of search engines.

Blogs are also a good source of online passive income. It gives the user freedom on creating their own content and lets them modify the appearance of their blog depending on their preferences or the audience they wish to attract. Since the dawn of the internet age, more and more people are now using blogs for personal usage or for profiting. In creating web content, blogs are commonly used by beginners since it saves them the time and money for coding and designs required for generating the site.

*If you love writing and enjoy all-types of writing, including article-writing, stories, movie scripts, and blogs be sure to check this out to earn good money.

Here are some blog creating sites for people interested in starting a blog:

Blogger

Blogger is a great tool for emerging and beginner authors. With it's easy to use features and interface; users won't even break a sweat when creating their first blog. It is one of the most popular blogging platforms today. After merging with Google, Blogger-supported websites definitely have higher chances of ranking in Google search pages.

Wordpress

Wordpress is a little complicated than Blogger. However,

in exchange for its complication, it gives the user full control of their blog. From coding to appearances, to widgets and plug-ins, more experienced bloggers tend to use Wordpress for its adaptability to the users' needs.

Blog.com

Blog.com is a friendly user blog website that offers a variety of upgrades. It lets the user own his/her own domain for $18 and allows multi-author blogs which lets the user pick a team of existing authors within the community to help in the creation of his/her blog, perfect for first time bloggers. The site also offers an advertisement feature, which allows the user to post clickable banner advertisements to further amplify earning potential.

WEEBLY

With its easy to use site builder, Weebly helps the user create professionally designed websites without the need for any technical experience. It also offers the 'eCommerce' website builder that is used to create a digital store for those interested selling digital goods, tangible products, and online services.

CREATING a blog today has never been this easy. Most blogging websites today offer a user-friendly experience wherein all the work of creating the website has been simplified for them. All the user needs to do is to create their content and share it to the world. However, once their content is up and running, it is only piled up on the millions of other blogs created by other people worldwide. That is why people whose intention to use the blog for making money online use SEO in order to escape from the pile.

TODAY PEOPLE ARE PUBLISHING Kindle Books online and making money at it. For more information, I highly recommend Michael Greene's Publish a Book In 14Days, where he takes you step by step to having a book written and published in only 14 days!

SEARCH ENGINE OPTIMIZATION

S EO or search engine optimization is a technique used by business minded individuals to improve page rankings on search engines, improving traffic. Users optimize their websites for high rankings given by the search engine such as Google, Yahoo! and Bing. Most blog creating sites offer these services to further retain their users and there are also some freelance companies specialized in SEO that offer their services for a fee.

Blogging and Article writing are very closely related. Article making saves the user the hassle from creating a website and gives the user the opportunity to focus more on how to write the best content possible. It can then be published online for free. However, it may take some time for the user to receive a decent amount of residual income since the earning potential depends on the number of articles published and the traffic each article gets.

Blogging grants the user freedom in creating a digital space wherein he/she is in command. In order to build a decent website, it is required to have a small initial capital. Also, it may require some SEO techniques in order for it to have more traffic, which if executed carefully, will generate a decent amount of passive income as well.

Both Blogging and Article writing require hard work in exchange for financial independence.

FIVERR.COM

A website that has blown up incredibly fast is www. fiverr.com. It is a website where you start out making $5 for any product or service you want to create. Each time you make a sale you earn $5 – some of the products/services can take as little as 5 minutes and as long as a few hours to create, depending on which service you choose to provide. After a month of good ratings you have the option to make much more money.

IF YOU'D LIKE to know how to easily get started, take a look at: *Ways To Make Money Using Fiverr.*

DAY TRADING, FOREX, AND INVESTING ONLINE

T hanks to the internet, anyone with a computer and an internet connection can now invest in the forex and stock market. But first, what are the forex market and the stock market? What are their differences? What are the pros and cons of both?

The forex market facilitates the buying and selling of currency, while the stock market facilitates the buying and selling of stocks. In forex, there are a lot of different determining factors on how currency rates fluctuate. But as with anything that can be sold in the world, its price is determined by the relationship between supply and demand. The more demand there is for the currency, the higher its price will be. The demand for a currency is affected by the following:

- The demand for goods, investments, or services being sold under that currency.
- Central banks sometimes buy a currency in order to decrease the difference between their own currency and the foreign currency being bought.

- Speculators will make educated predictions on how the currency rates will change in the future, directly affecting the demand for the currencies.

The forex market is characterized with high liquidity, especially through online trading sites. This means a currency can be sold or bought quickly. The forex market also operates at 24 hours a day, except during weekends while the stock market opens and closes at a set time. While the forex market facilitates trades in currency, the stock market allows people to buy 'pieces' of a company called a 'stock'. Individuals who own stocks are cold stockholders. These stocks are issued by the company in order to get funding and as the worth of the company increases, the value of stocks increase as well. Stocks can appreciate or depreciate over time. Making money in stocks can be a lot harder than making money in forex.

An excellent book for getting started in the Forex Market by Todd Williams. It takes you through the do's and don'ts of the forex market so you can make money, not lose it!

ONLINE TRADING WEBSITES

Forex and stock trading in the internet could be very confusing at first. In order to get started, you must first be educated about how the markets work. There are free online courses that you can take if want to know more about forex and stock trading. There is so much to learn in order for you to profit from these markets. You must be familiar with the terms or trade policies in order for you to make an educated prediction of how the market will move. As always, if you want to make money online through forex and stocks, you must invest a lot of time in learning the basics.

Some websites allow their users to 'follow' another trader, with a list of the most successful traders that can be followed. This means he can copy the trades of that person, which is probably a good bet. Online currency and stock exchanges opened up a way for anyone to invest in markets from their homes. Here is a list of the most reputable forex and stock trading websites:

1. eToro – www.etoro.com
2. Instaforex – www.instaforex.com
3. STO – www.supertradingonline.com
4. Easy forex – www.easyforex.com
5. Trade King – www.tradeking.com
6. Fidelity Investments – www.fidelity.com
7. Scottrade – www.scottrade.com
8. FXCM Micro – www.forexmicrolot.com
9. Swissquote – www.swissquote.com
10. Forex Yard – www.forexyard.com
11. Forex Realm – www.forexrealm.com
12. E*Trade – www.etrade.com
13. Crown forex – www.crownforex.com
14. CitiFX Pro – www.citifxpro.com
15. TD Ameritrade – www.tdameritrade.com

INVESTING in the forex and stock market even at home may take a long time to learn and can be frustrating. Also, the returns may not be as great with smaller investments. But, investing in the forex or stock market is more advisable than opening a savings account in a bank. The interest you get from a savings account is too small to give substantial results, usually less than 5% annually.

IF YOU WANT to get more specific and build your investment portfolio faster with Stock Trading, take a look at these simple guides to Binary Options and Currency Trading. One word of caution is to always do your research when beginning Online Trading because even though you can potentially make a lot of money fast, thee are still scams out there.

RENT OUT YOUR LIVING SPACE, MAKE MONEY, AND TRAVEL

One website that has gotten very popular over the past year and completely changed the world of renting is **www.airbnb.com**.

IT IS a site where you can take your living space – whether it be a house, condo, room, or closet in San Francisco – and charge for it. Guests from all around the world will inquire about your living space, and you can charge any price you'd like (of course making it competitive with the other **www. airbnb.com** listings). Then you get to choose who you want to be in your room, based on their online profile and past user rating.

THAT WAY you anytime you want to travel, you can simply rent out your living area (to cover the rent, and maybe even part of your travel expenses). It is worth taking a look if you enjoy traveling, or want to make some extra income.

THE KEYS TO BUILDING WEALTH

U *nderstanding Assets and Liabilities*

THE KEY to building wealth whether or not by online means, is to understand the difference between assets and liabilities. The definition of an asset in terms of accounting is an item of value that you own. While this is technically correct, a small change in your mindset and a slight change in the way you look at assets can be a huge difference. In terms of accounting, a car or a house, assuming that you own them, is an asset. Then it is to be accepted that cellphones, gadgets, or tablets are assets, right? Again, this is technically correct. But consider changing your definition of assets. Think of assets simply as something that generates revenue, and think of liabilities simply as something that contributes to your expenses. With this kind of mindset, re-think about the previous examples. A car is something you need for transportation, but does it does not directly generate income by itself, unless if you're a taxi driver. A car may get you places but it costs you money too. Not just the money you spent on purchasing the car, but also the gas costs that you've paid in order to use it. It doesn't mean that you should not invest in a car or a house. This just represents a much wider and newer perspective on how assets and liabilities can be seen.

As with liabilities, this could be anything that costs you money. Your education is a liability, your electricity and water consumption bills are liabilities, your girlfriend could be a liability too, and so on. Just remember that it is completely normal to have liabilities. As long as you have assets that can cover the costs.

In simple mathematics, **assets - liabilities = profit/loss**. You profit if your assets are bigger than your liabilities, and you lose money if your liabilities are bigger than your assets.

In the previous chapters of this e-book, you were presented with details about virtual assets such as domain names, articles, videos, and other forms of investments. You can consider all of those as assets. The secret to becoming rich is investing more on assets than liabilities. Save money to invest online, open a small business, or invest in other small businesses. Keep on investing so that your assets will devour all your liabilities. This is the key to building wealth.

Debts and Savings

If you find yourself buried in debt, there is one thing that you can and should do immediately: stop getting into more debts and actually start paying. Paying debts as early as you can will not only save you from interests, but will also save you the stress that can result from debts. It is important to avoid too much debt. Commit yourself into using just one credit card, and no more. As stated earlier, invest in assets, not liabilities.

Keep a record of your debts and keep them organized. Start keeping a record of your earnings and your expenses. Always think twice when purchasing something. Sell the things that you no longer need. Open a yard sale, or sell them on eBay, whatever you can to earn money while abstaining from buying unnecessary things.

Sometimes people tend to ignore the coins lying around in their houses. Or sometimes we want to impress other people by saying, 'keep the change'. This may indeed be impressive, but be wise. People often underestimate the amount they can save from coins and change. The next time you see a quarter, pick it up and keep it in a jar. Do this for every coin you find, pretty soon the jar will be full and you'll be surprised on the amount you've saved in there.

SHORTCUTS RICH PEOPLE USE TO
BECOME WEALTHY

A lot of people believe that there is a secret that only rich people know, a 'shortcut' to riches and financial freedom. These people often buy into get-rich-quick schemes and lose a lot of time finding the 'secret'.

The truth is, there is a secret, but there are no shortcuts. However there are things you can do to gain wealth faster. Success is not something you gain without hard work; unless of course if you're extremely lucky and win the lottery or discover a gold deposit under your house.

The only thing rich people know that others don't is how to commit to their business and work hard consistently. A lot of people give up when things get tough or when they fail to see results. Failure is inevitable, but not everybody has the persistence to keep going. Be passionate about your financial welfare. Start investing, and spend less; this is all you need to remember. Do not be afraid of risk, but do not forget to calculate and manage them well.

Finally, never give up and continue to learn. Over time

you will learn from experience how to invest well. Most of these investments can be done at home, thanks to the internet. Use this to your advantage.

AFTERWORD

The internet could be one of the most important inventions ever to be conceived by mankind. It opened endless possibilities that changed and continue to change the world of communications, education, military, politics, business, and science. Information is everything, and the world is full of it. With the power of the internet, anyone with a computer, internet connection, and the will to learn, can become financially successful.

Always remember to never give up, for it is not with each success, but with each failure that you can become a better businessman, entrepreneur, and a much stronger person.

Overall, I hope you were able to use this book to get some great ideas, resources, and knowledge to begin living the life you want to live.

www.ingramcontent.com/pod-product-compliance
Lightning Source LLC
Chambersburg PA
CBHW071532210326
41597CB00018B/2975